This Coloring Book

A Child of God

This coloring book is a special journey into understanding and embracing the incredible truth of who you are in Christ.

As you color each page, take time to meditate on the powerful Bible verses that speak directly to your identity in Him. These verses are reminders that you are loved, chosen, and redeemed. You belong to Him, and nothing can change that.

Each coloring page is printed on a single side to prevent bleed-through.

Let this book be more than just a creative outlet; let it be a moment of reflection and connection with the One who made you and calls you His own.
Let Him, and let that truth fill your heart with peace, joy, and confidence.
You are wonderfully made, deeply loved, and have a purpose in Christ.

Embrace who you are in Him, and let that truth fill your heart with peace, joy, and confidence.

This book is lovingly dedicated to my dear niece and nephew, Kareana and Jonathan. May you always know who you are in Christ and find strength, joy, and purpose in His love. You are each a beautiful reminder of God's grace and blessings in my life.

With all my love...

Romans 8:2

For the law of the Spirit of life in Christ Jesus has made me free from the law of sin and death.

Reflect on how Christ's freedom changes your perspective on guilt and fear.

How can you live in that freedom today?

You are free from condemnation!

For the law of the Spirit of life in Christ Jesus hath made me free from the law of sin and death. - Romans 8:2

15 For we do not have a high priest who is unable to empathize with our weaknesses, but we have one who has been tempted in every way, just as we are—yet he did not sin. 16 Let us then approach God's throne of grace with confidence, so that we may receive mercy and find grace to help us in our time of need. -Hebrews 4:15-16

And we know that all things work together for good to them that love God, to them who are the called according to his purpose.
-Romans 8:28

I am the vine, ye are the branches: He that abideth in me, and I in him, the same bringeth forth much fruit: for without me ye can do nothing. - John 15:5

Hebrews 4: 15-16

15 For we do not have a high priest who is unable to empathize with our weaknesses, but we have one who has been tempted in every way, just as we are—yet he did not sin. 16 Let us then approach God's throne of grace with confidence, so that we may receive mercy and find grace to help us in our time of need.

Consider a recent challenge or temptation. How does knowing that Jesus understands your struggles help you seek God's grace and mercy with confidence?

Romans 8:28

And we know that all things work together for good to them that love God, to them who are the called according to his purpose.

Think about a challenging situation. How can you trust that God is working it for your good?

God works in favor of you in all circumstances!

John 15:5

I am the vine, ye are the branches: He that abideth in me, and I in him, the same bringeth forth much fruit: for without me ye can do nothing.

How can you stay connected to Christ today? What fruit do you hope to see in your life as a result?

You are a bracnch of Jesus Christ, the true vine!

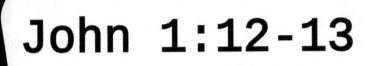

John 1:12-13

But as many as received him, to them gave he power to become the sons of God, even to them that believe on his name: 13 Which were born, not of blood, nor of the will of the flesh, nor of the will of man, but of God.

What does it mean to you to be a child of God? How does this identity shape your life?

You are a child of God!

12 But as many as received him, to them gave he power to become the sons of God, even to them that believe on his name:
13 Which were born, not of blood, nor of the will of the flesh, nor of the will of man, but of God. - John 1:12-13

But he that is joined unto the Lord is one spirit. -1 Corinthians 6:17

Ye have not chosen me, but I have chosen you, and ordained you, that ye should go and bring forth fruit, and that your fruit should remain: that whatsoever ye shall ask of the Father in my name, he may give it you.
- John 15:16

5 Even when we were dead in sins, hath quickened us together with Christ, (by grace ye are saved;)
6 And hath raised us up together, and made us sit together in heavenly places in Christ Jesus. - Ephesians 2:5-6

1 Corinthians 6:17

But he that is joined unto the Lord is one spirit.

Consider what it means to be one with the Lord in spirit. How does this union influence your thoughts, actions, and decisions?

You are united with the Lord and you are one with Him in Spirit!

John 15:16

Ye have not chosen me, but I have chosen you, and ordained you, that ye should go and bring forth fruit, and that your fruit should remain: that whatsoever ye shall ask of the Father in my name, he may give it you.

How does knowing God chose and appointed you, change your actions? What lasting fruit do you hope to bear?

You are are chosen by God!

Ephesians 2:5-6

Even when we were dead in sins, hath quickened us together with Christ, (by grace ye are saved;) 6 And hath raised us up together, and made us sit together in heavenly places in Christ Jesus:

How does God's grace make you feel alive in Christ? What does being seated with Him in heavenly places mean to you?
You are seated with Jesus Christ!

Colossians 2:9-10

For in him dwelleth all the fulness of the Godhead bodily.
10 And ye are complete in him, which is the head of all principality and power:

What does it mean to be brought to fullness in Christ? How does His authority shape your life?

You are complete in Christ!

9 For in him dwelleth all the fulness of the Godhead bodily.
10 And ye are complete in him, which is the head of all principality and power:
- Colossians 2:9-10

10 For we are his workmanship, created in Christ Jesus unto good works, which God hath before ordained that we should walk in them. - Ephesians 2:10

21 Now he which stablisheth us with you in Christ, and hath anointed us, is God;
22 Who hath also sealed us, and given the earnest of the Spirit in our hearts.
- 2 Corinthians 1:21-22

20 Now then, we are ambassadors for Christ, as though God were pleading through us: we implore you on Christ's behalf, be reconciled to God. 21 For He made Him who knew no sin to be sin for us, that we might become the righteousness of God in Him.
- 2 Corinthians 5:20-21

Ephesians 2:10

For we are his workmanship, created in Christ Jesus unto good works, which God hath before ordained that we should walk in them.

How can you live out the good works God has prepared for you? In what ways do you see yourself as God's handiwork?

You are God's workmanship!

2 Corinthians 1:21-22

21 Now he which stablisheth us with you in Christ, and hath anointed us, is God; 22 Who hath also sealed us, and given the earnest of the Spirit in our hearts.

How does knowing you are sealed and anointed by God give you confidence?

You are annointed and Sealed by God!

2 Corinthians 5:20-21

Now then we are ambassadors for Christ, as though God did beseech you by us: we pray you in Christ's stead, be ye reconciled to God.21 For he hath made him to be sin for us, who knew no sin; that we might be made the righteousness of God in him.

What does it mean to be Christ's ambassador?

You are an ambassador for Christ!

Philippians 3:20

But our citizenship is in heaven. And we eagerly await a Savior from there, the Lord Jesus Christ,

How does knowing your true citizenship is in heaven influence your choices and priorities? In what ways can you live with a heavenly perspective today?
You are a citizen of Heaven!

But our citizenship is in heaven. And we eagerly await a Savior from there, the Lord Jesus Christ, - Philippians 3:20

13 For he has rescued us from the dominion of darkness and brought us into the kingdom of the Son he loves, 14 in whom we have redemption, the forgiveness of sins. - Colossians 1:13-14

Trust in the Lord with all your heart and lean not on your own understanding; 6 in all your ways submit to him, and he will make your paths straight. - Proverbs 3:5-6

In him and through faith in him we may approach God with freedom and confidence. - Ephesians 3:12

Colossians 1:13-14

13 For he has rescued us from the dominion of darkness and brought us into the kingdom of the Son he loves, 14 in whom we have redemption, the forgiveness of sins.

How does it feel to be rescued and redeemed by Christ? How can you live in the light of His kingdom today?

You are forgiven and redeemed of sins!

Proverbs 3:5-6

Trust in the Lord with all your heart
and lean not on your own understanding;
6 in all your ways submit to him,
and he will make your paths straight.

How can trusting in the Lord guide
your sense of identity in Christ?

In what areas of your life do you
need to lean on His understanding
rather than your own?

Ephesians 3:12

In him and through faith in him we may approach God with freedom and confidence.

How does your faith in Christ give you confidence to approach God boldly?

You can approach God with freedom and confidence!

Romans 5:1

Therefore, since we have been justified through faith, we have peace with God through our Lord Jesus Christ,

How does being justified through faith give you peace with God? In what areas in your life can you find more peace?

You have been justified!

Therefore, since we have been justified through faith, we have peace with God through our Lord Jesus Christ, - Romans: 5:1

Now you are the body of Christ, and each one of you is a part of it. - 1 Corinthians 12:27

1 Since, then, you have been raised with Christ, set your hearts on things above, where Christ is, seated at the right hand of God. 2 Set your minds on things above, not on earthly things. 3 For you died, and your life is now hidden with Christ in God. 4 When Christ, who is your life, appears, then you also will appear with him in glory. - Colossians 3:1-4

For God hath not given us the spirit of fear; but of power, and of love, and of a sound mind. - 2 Timothy 1:7

1 Corinthians 12:27

Now you are the body of Christ, and each one of you is a part of it.

How do you see your role in the body of Christ?

What are ways you can contribute to the the body of Christ?

You are a part of Christ's body!

Colossians 3:1-4

3 Since, then, you have been raised with Christ, set your hearts on things above, where Christ is, seated at the right hand of God. 2 Set your minds on things above, not on earthly things. 3 For you died, and your life is now hidden with Christ in God. 4 When Christ, who is your life, appears, then you also will appear with him in glory.

What does it mean to set your heart and mind on the things above? How can you focus more on your life in Christ today?

You are hidden with Christ in God!

2 Timothy 1:7

For God hath not given us the spirit of fear; but of power, and of love, and of a sound mind.

How can you embrace the power, love, and a sound mind that God has given you? What steps can you take to overcome fear with His strength today?

You have not been given a spirit of fear. You have been given power, love and a sound mind!

Philippians 1:6-7

6 Being confident of this very thing, that he which hath begun a good work in you will perform it until the day of Jesus Christ: 7 Even as it is meet for me to think this of you all, because I have you in my heart; inasmuch as both in my bonds, and in the defence and confirmation of the gospel, ye all are partakers of my grace.

How does knowing that God will complete the good work He started in you give you confidence? In what ways can you trust His ongoing work in your life today?

God will complete the good work He started in you!

6 Being confident of this very thing, that he which hath begun a good work in you will perform it until the day of Jesus Christ: 7 Even as it is meet for me to think this of you all, because I have you in my heart; inasmuch as both in my bonds, and in the defence and confirmation of the gospel, ye all are partakers of my grace.

- Philippians 1:6-7

We know that anyone born of God does not continue to sin; the One who was born of God keeps them safe, and the evil one cannot harm them. - 1 John 5:18

I can do all things through Christ which strengtheneth me. - Philippians 4:13

31 What, then, shall we say in response to these things? If God is for us, who can be against us? 32 He who did not spare his own Son, but gave him up for us all—how will he not also, along with him, graciously give us all things? - Romans 8:31-32

1 John 5:18

We know that anyone born of God does not continue to sin; the One who was born of God keeps them safe, and the evil one cannot harm them.

How does being born of God empower you to live righteously? In what ways can you trust God's protection against evil?

You are born of God and evil cannot harm you!

Philippians 4:13

I can do all this through him who gives me strength.

The verse is more about being content and enduring all circumstances — good or bad — through Christ's strength, rather than achieving anything you desire.

Philippians 4:13 reminds us that Christ provides strength in every situation. Think of an area in your life where you need His strength today. Pray for Christ's help in facing this area in your life with faith and perseverance.

Romans 8:31-32

31 What, then, shall we say in response to these things? If God is for us, who can be against us? 32 He who did not spare his own Son, but gave him up for us all—how will he not also, along with him, graciously give us all things?

How does knowing that God is for you give you confidence? What challenges can you face with the assurance that He is on your side?

God is with you!

Zephaniah 3:17

The Lord your God is with you,the Mighty Warrior who saves.
He will take great delight in you; in his love he will no longer rebuke you,
but will rejoice over you with singing.

How does it comfort you to know that God rejoices over you? In what ways can you rest in His love today?

The Lord is delighted in you!

The Lord your God is with you, the Mighty Warrior who saves.
He will take great delight in you; in his love he will no longer rebuke you, but will rejoice over you with singing.
- Zephaniah 3:17

When I called, you answered me; you greatly emboldened me. - Psalms 138:3

3 Praise be to the God and Father of our Lord Jesus Christ, who has blessed us in the heavenly realms with every spiritual blessing in Christ. - Ephesians 1:3

4 For he chose us in him before the creation of the world to be holy and blameless in his sight. In love 5 he predestined us for adoption to sonship through Jesus Christ, in accordance with his pleasure and will— - Ephesians 1:4-5

Psalm 138:3

When I called, you answered me;
    you greatly emboldened me.

When has God answered you in a time of need? How has His strength supported you in difficult moments?

God will always answer you!

Ephesians 1:3

Praise be to the God and Father of our Lord Jesus Christ, who has blessed us in the heavenly realms with every spiritual blessing in Christ.

What spiritual blessings have you received in Christ? How can you live in gratitude for these blessings today?

God has blessed you in the heavenly realms!

Ephesians 1:4-5

4 For he chose us in him before the creation of the world to be holy and blameless in his sight. In love 5 he predestined us for adoption to sonship through Jesus Christ, in accordance with his pleasure and will-

How does knowing you were chosen by God before the world began impact your sense of purpose? What does being adopted into His family mean to you?

You are chosen by God and adopted as His child!

1 Corinthians 2:9

But as it is written: "Eye has not seen, nor ear heard,
Nor have entered into the heart of man
The things which God has prepared for those who love Him.

What great things do you believe God has prepared for you? How can you trust in His wonderful plans for your life?

God has great things planned for your life!

But as it is written:
Eye has not seen, nor ear heard,
Nor have entered into the heart of man
The things which God has prepared for those
who love Him. - 1 Corinthians 2:9

29 Are not two sparrows sold for a copper coin? And not one of them falls to the ground apart from your Father's will. 30 But the very hairs of your head are all numbered. 31 Do not fear therefore; you are of more value than many sparrows. - Matthew 10:29-31

Matthew 10:29-31

29 Are not two sparrows sold for a copper coin? And not one of them falls to the ground apart from your Father's will. 30 But the very hairs of your head are all numbered. 31 Do not fear therefore; you are of more value than many sparrows.

How does understanding your value to God bring you comfort?

You are very important to God!

Reflection

Reflection

Reflection

Reflection

Made in United States
Troutdale, OR
04/13/2025